GOD'S
PASSION
FOR YOU

BILLY GRAHAM

MAX LUCADO

ANNE GRAHAM LOTZ

JOHN MACARTHUR

CHARLES SWINDOLL

COUNTRYMAN
A Division of Thomas Nelson Publishers

THOMAS NELSON
Since 1798

NASHVILLE   MEXICO CITY   RIO DE JANEIRO

Designed by DesignWorks, Sisters, Oregon

ISBN: 978-1-4041-0237-8

Printed in the United States

14 15 16 17 18 POL 5 4 3 2

INTRODUCTION

World in Pain

In my travels over the decades, I have found that people are the same the world over. However, in recent years I find that there is an increasing problem that I would sum up in the word "hopeless." It may be because we get the news of troubles, problems, disasters, wars, etc. instantaneously in comparison to years ago when it might have taken weeks, months, or even years to hear of an event. But there's something else even more insidious. People in the most affluent societies are feeling this sense of despair and hopelessness.

Perhaps the greatest psychological, spiritual, and medical need that all people have is the need for hope. Dr. McNair Wilson, the famous cardiologist, remarked in his autobiography, *Doctor's Progress*, "Hope is the medicine I use more than any other—hope can cure nearly anything."

I remember years ago that Dr. Harold Wolff, professor of medicine at Cornell University Medical College and associate professor of psychiatry, said, "Hope, like faith and a purpose in life, is medicinal. This is not exactly a statement of belief, but a conclusion proved by meticulously controlled scientific experiment."

Voices from Troubled Hearts:

"Our home is a war zone! Don't talk to me about international war. I want to know how we can find peace in our family!". . . "I'm a rape victim. How can I ever get over my memories, or my horrible fears?" . . . "I've lost my job and may lose my home. Don't tell me about Wall Street blues!" . . . "How can I raise decent kids when they're the most endangered species!" . . . "We have a nice home and car—you'd think I would be happy. But I feel empty.

I'm not sure of my husband anymore and I'm so lonely."

"This is the generation that will pass through the fire. It is the generation . . . 'under the gun.' This is the tormented generation. This is the generation destined to live in the midst of crisis, danger, fear, and death. We are like a people under sentence of death, waiting for the date to be set. We sense that something is about to happen. We know that things cannot go on as they are. History has reached an impasse. We are now on a collision course. Something is about to give."

I wrote this in 1965!

At that time few of us thought that the world could get much worse and survive. I was wrong. In many ways the world has gotten worse, and we have survived. But we are a world in pain—a world that suffers collectively from the violence of nature and man, and a world that suffers individually from personal heartache.

Because we have instant communication today, our planet has shrunk to the size of a television screen. Although husbands and wives, children and parents, have trouble communicating, we can watch a war as it is happening before our eyes. A comfortable room can be turned into a foreign battlefield or a street riot with the push of a button.

Someone has said that Americans have more wealth, more two-car families, more private homes, and write more books on how to be happy than any other country. If we lived in Bangladesh or in the slums of Calcutta, the thought of suffering in the midst of abundance would sound ridiculous. And yet in America, where the standard of living is one of the highest in the world, the very presence of a life of comparative ease causes a spiritual sickness.

When suffering hits us personally, that is the common cry. *Why Me? What's the reason?* For man without faith in a personal God, reactions to painful situations are as varied as pain itself. Without God's guidance, our response to suffering is a futile attempt to find solutions to conditions that cannot be solved. We are plummeting into a world where, in spite of wonder drugs and medical breakthroughs, suffering will become more intense. For all suffering, we know, is not physical. Today, more than ever, we need to know how to find strength to live life to its fullest.

Some see God as a harsh father, waiting to punish His children when they do something wrong. Others perceive God as unable to handle the evil on earth, or indifferent to the suffering caused by it.

God's Unfailing Love

God's love is unchangeable; He knows exactly what we are and loves us anyway. In fact, He created us because He wanted other creatures in His image upon whom He could pour out His love and who would love Him in return. He also wanted that love to be voluntary, not forced, so He gave us freedom of choice, the ability to say yes or no in our relationship to Him. God does not want mechanized love, the kind that says we must love God because it's what our parents demand or our church preaches. Only voluntary love satisfies the Heart of God.

On the human level, we frequently love the one who loves us. In the spiritual realm, people do not grasp the overwhelming love of a holy God, but we can understand God's love getting to know Him through Jesus Christ. No one can grasp the love of God of the universe without knowing His Son.

BILLY GRAHAM, *Hope for the Troubled Heart*

God's Passion for You

The movie, The Passion of the Christ revealed the horror of what God's Son, Jesus Christ suffered. You may even be one of those individuals who wondered Why? . . . Why would Jesus endure such pain and agony especially if he is the Son of God. Or perhaps you don't believe it really happened or maybe you have a tiny bit of belief but something is holding you back from really believing.

First, let's look at a verse in the Bible that was written about 700 years before Christ was born. In the Old Testament book of Isaiah, God inspired the writer to pen these words in the 52nd Chapter:

Many were amazed when they saw him—beaten and bloodied, so disfigured one would scarcely know he was a person. Then continued in the 53rd chapter . . . *He was oppressed and treated harshly yet he never said a word. He was led as a lamb to the slaughter. And as a sheep is silent before the shearers, he did not open his mouth. From prison and trial they led him away to his death. But who among the people realized that he was dying for their sins—that He was suffering their punishment. He had done no wrong and he never deceived anyone . . . and because of what he experienced, my righteous servant will make it possible for many to be counted righteous, for He will bear all their sins* (NLT).

REMEMBER: these words were written 700 years before Christ came to earth.

BOTTOM LINE: God loves you so much that he sent his only son, Jesus Christ to take your due punishment and in return give you abundant life and life everlasting.

In the Bible Jesus says in the book of John Chapter 3 verse 16,

For God so loved the world that He gave His only begotten Son, that whoever believes in Him should not perish but have everlasting life . . . and then in John 10:10, Jesus says, *I have come that they may have life, and that they may have it more abundantly* (NKJV).

Jesus Forgives You

The hand squeezing the handle was not a Roman infantryman. The force behind the hammer was not an angry mob. The verdict behind the death was not decided by jealous Jews. Jesus Himself chose the nails. So the hands of Jesus opened up. Had the soldier hesitated, Jesus Himself would have swung the mallet. He knew how; He was no stranger to the driving of nails. As a carpenter He knew what it took. And as a Savior He knew what it meant. He knew that the purpose of the nail was to place your sins where they could be hidden by His sacrifice and covered by His blood.

MAX LUCADO, *Experiencing the Heart of Jesus*

Can you imagine someone loving you so much that they would die for you? Scripture continues to reveals God's love for you in the book of Romans chapter 8 verses 38–39 . . .

neither death nor life, nor angels nor principalities nor powers, nor things present nor things to come, nor height nor depth, nor any other created thing, shall be able to separate us from the love of God which is in Christ Jesus our Lord (NKJV).

The Message of the Two Crosses

Jesus' forgiveness is a done deal, accomplished at Calvary. However, "Calvary's trio" of the crosses reminds us we must personally accept that and embrace this gift in our lives.

Ever wonder why there were two crosses next to Christ? Why not six or ten? Ever wonder why Jesus was in the center? Why not on the far right or far left? Could it be that the two crosses on the hill symbolize one of God's greatest gifts? The gift of choice.

The two criminals have so much in common. Convicted by the same system. Condemned to the same death. Surrounded by the same crowd. Equally close to the same Jesus. In fact, they begin with the same sarcasm: "The two criminals also said cruel things to Jesus."

But one changed.

One of the criminals on a cross began to shout insults at Jesus: "Aren't you the Christ? Then save yourself and us." But the other criminal stopped him and said, "You should fear God! You are getting the same punishment he is. We are punished justly, getting what we deserve for what we did. But this man has done nothing wrong." Then he said, "Jesus, remember me when you come into your kingdom." Jesus said to him, *"I tell you the truth, today you will be with me in paradise."*

Much has been said about the prayer of the penitent thief, and it certainly warrants our admiration. But while we rejoice at the thief who changed, dare we forget the one who didn't? What about him, Jesus? Wouldn't a personal invitation be appropriate? Wouldn't a word of persuasion be timely?

There are times when God sends thunder to stir us. There are times when God sends blessings to lure us. But there are times when God sends nothing but silence as he honors us with the freedom to choose where we spend eternity.

Have we been given any greater privilege than that of choice? Not only does this privilege offset any injustice, the gift of free will can offset any mistakes.

Think about the thief who repented. Though we know little about him, we know this: He made some bad mistakes in life. He chose the wrong crowd, the wrong morals, the wrong behavior. But would you consider his life a waste? Is he spending eternity reaping the fruit of all the bad choices he made? No, just the opposite. He is enjoying the fruit of one good choice he made. In the end all his bad choices were redeemed by a solitary good one.

No matter how many bad choices you have made in the past, they are redeemed by one good choice—to follow Jesus. Will you make that choice now? Not only will your life be impacted for eternity but your life on earth will have purpose.

Jesus says, *"Here I am! I stand at the door and knock. If anyone hears my voice and opens the door, I will come in . . ."* (Revelation 3:20 NIV).

Why don't you start with your bad moments? Those bad habits? Leave them at the Cross. Your selfish moods and white lies? Give them to God. Your binges and bigotries? God wants them all. Every flop, every failure. He wants every single one. Why? Because he knows we can't live with them.

MAX LUCADO, *Experiencing the Heart of Jesus*

With all of my heart, I urge you accept God's purpose for your life. According to the Bible, "*Jesus is the only One who can save people. His name is the only power in the world that has been given to save people. We must be saved through him.*" (Acts 4:12 NCV)

Would you let him save you? This is the most important decision you will ever make. Why don't you give your heart to him right now? Admit your need. *If we confess our sins to him, his faithful and just to forgive us and to cleanse us from every wrong"* (1 John 1:9 NLT). Agree that Jesus died to pay for your sins and that he rose from the dead and is alive today. "*If you confess with your mouth, 'Jesus is Lord,' and believe in your heart that God raised him from the dead, you will be saved"* (Romans 10:9 NIV). Accept God's free gift of salvation. Don't try to earn it. *"For it is by grace you have been saved, through faith—and this is not from yourselves, it is the gift of God—not by works, so that no one can boast"* (Ephesians 2:8–9 NIV). *"But as many as received Him to them He gave the right to become children of God, to those who believe in His name: who were born, not of blood, nor of the will of the flesh, nor of the will of man, but of God* (John 1:12–13 NKJV).

MAX LUCADO, *He Did This Just for You*

Go to God in prayer and tell him, *I am a sinner in need of grace. I believe that Jesus died for me on the cross. I accept your offer of salvation.* It's a simple prayer with eternal results.

YOUR RESPONSE

I believe that Jesus Christ is the Son of the Living God. I want him to be the Lord of my life.

SIGNED_____

DATE _____

The Hope of the Not Yet

He is building a house for you. And with every swing of the hammer and cut of the saw, he's dreaming of the day he carries you over the threshold. *"There are many rooms in my Father's house; I would not tell you this if it were not true. I am going there to prepare a place for you. After I go and prepare a place for you, I will come back take you to be with me so that you may be where I am"* (John 14:2–3 NCV).

MAX LUCADO, *Experiencing the Heart of Jesus*

God's Mission: Adoption

When we come to Christ, God not only forgives us, he also adopts us. Through a dramatic series of events, we go from condemned orphans with no hope to be adopted children with no fear. Here is how it happens. You come before the judgment seat of God full of rebellion and mistakes. Because of his justice he cannot dismiss your sin, but because of his love he cannot dismiss you. So, in an act which stunned the heavens, he punished himself on the cross for your sins. God's justice and love are equally honored. And you, God's creation, are forgiven. But the story doesn't end with God's forgiveness.

For you have not received a spirit of slavery leading to fear again, but you have received a spirit of adoption as sons by which we cry out "Abba! Father!" The Spirit himself bears witness with our Spirit that we are children God (Romans 8:15–16 NASB).

But when the fullness of time came, God sent forth His Son, born of a woman, born under the Law, in order that He might redeem those who were under the Law, that we might receive the adoption as sons (Galatians 4:4–5 NASB).

It would be enough if God just cleansed your name, but he does more. He gives you his name. It would be enough if God just set you free, but he does more. He takes you home. He takes you home to the Great House of God.

Adoptive parents understand this more than anyone. They know what it means to feel an empty space inside. They know what it means to hunt, to set out on a mission, and take responsibility for a child with a spotted past and dubious future.

God has adopted you. God sought you, found you, signed the papers and took you home.

Delight in these words:

Long ago, even before he made the world, God loved us and chose us in Christ to be holy and without fault in his eyes. His unchanging plan has always been to adopt us into his own family by bringing us to himself through Jesus Christ. And this gave him great pleasure. (Ephesians 1:3–5 NLT)

And you thought God adopted you because you were

good looking. You thought he needed your money or your wisdom. Sorry. God adopted you simply because he wanted to.

You were in his good will and pleasure. Knowing full well the trouble you would be and the price he would pay, he signed his name next to yours and changed your name to his and took you home. Your Abba adopted you and became your Father.

You and I both know that an adoption is not something we earn; it's something we receive. To be adopted into a family is not a feat one achieves, but rather a gift one accepts.

The parents are the active ones. Adoption agencies don't train children to recruit parents; they seek parents to adopt children. The parents make the call and fill out the papers and endure the interviews and pay the fee and wait and wait. Can you imagine prospective parents saying, "We'd like to adopt Johnny, but first we want to know a few things. Does he have a house to live in? Does he have money for tuition? Does he have a ride to school every morning and clothes to wear every day? Can he prepare his own meals and mend his own clothes?"

No agency would stand for such talk. Its representative would lift her hand and say, "Wait a minute. You don't understand. You don't adopt Johnny because of what he has; you adopt him because of what he needs. He needs a home."

The same is true with God. He doesn't adopt us because of what we have. He doesn't give us his name because of our wit or wallet or good attitude. Paul states it twice because he is doubly concerned that we understand that adoption is something we receive, not something we earn.

God is no fair-weather Father. He's not into this love-'em-and-leave-'em- stuff. I can count on him to be in my corner no matter how I perform. You can too.

Your Father will never turn you away. It is right to call him Holy; we speak truth when we call him King. But if you want to touch his heart, use the name he loves to hear. Call him Father.

MAX LUCADO, *The Great House of God*

On the following pages are twenty daily
devotions to help you as you begin your
new life and scripture verses to help you in
your new life. We encourage you to
experience the magnificent love God has for
you by reading the whole story. Obtain a
Bible and discover all that God has
purposed for your life.

Hope
for Each Day

Words of Wisdom and Faith

Billy Graham

The Tug of God's Love

*The Spirit Himself bears witness with our spirit that
we are children of God.*

ROMANS 8:16 NKJV

 Whenever anyone asks me how I can be so certain
about who and what God really is, I am reminded
of the story of the little boy who was out flying a kite. It
was a fine day for kite flying, the wind was brisk and large
billowy clouds were blowing across the sky. The kite went
up and up until it was entirely hidden by the clouds.

"What are you doing?" a man asked the little boy.

"I'm flying a kite," he replied.

"Flying a kite?" the man said. "How can you be sure?
You can't see the kite."

"No," said the boy, "I can't see it, but every little while
I feel a tug, so I know for sure that it's there!"

Don't take anyone else's word for God. Find Him for
yourself by inviting Jesus Christ to come into your life.
Then you, too, will know by the wonderful, warm tug on
your heartstrings that He is there *for sure*.

Love Demonstrated

He loved us and sent His Son
to be the propitiation for our sins.

1 JOHN 4:10 NKJV

The word *love* is used to mean many different things. We say that we "love" the house that we have just bought or that we "love" a particular vacation spot or that we "love" a peanut butter and jelly sandwich. We also "love" a certain television program, and we "love" our husband or wife. Hopefully we don't love our spouse the same way we love a peanut butter and jelly sandwich!

The greatest love of all, however, is God's love for us—a love that showed itself in action. A friend once observed, "Love talked about is easily ignored, but love demonstrated is irresistible." The Bible says "God demonstrates His own love toward us, in that while we were still sinners, Christ died for us" (Romans 5:8). Now that is *real* love! How will you respond to His love today?

Christ Provides the Cure

If anyone is in Christ, he is a new creation.

2 CORINTHIANS 5:17 NKJV

Wouldn't it be wonderful if we could find a medicine that would absolutely cure human nature's weaknesses and failures? Conflict, discontent, and unhappiness plague people everywhere. But suppose a cure could be found for humanity's ills. It would cause a worldwide stampede!

The most thrilling news in the world is that there is a cure! God has provided the medicine—and that "medicine" is Christ. Through Him our sins can be forgiven, and by His Holy Spirit within us our lives can be changed and renewed.

Sin, confusion, and disillusionment can be replaced by righteousness, joy, and hope. Our souls can know peace, a peace that is not dependent on outward circumstances. This cure was provided two thousand years ago by Jesus Christ's death and resurrection for us. Is He working daily in your life, changing you and making you more like Him?

No Bargain, No Barter

Come, buy, . . . without money
and without price.

ISAIAH 55:1 NKJV

God does not bargain with us, nor can we barter with Him. He holds our eternal salvation in His omnipotent hand, and He bids us take it as a free gift, "without money and without price."

Yet this is hard for us to accept. Surely something as precious as salvation must cost us greatly! Surely God must demand we work for it!

But that is wrong—and the reason is because the price has already been paid! Salvation is free—but it wasn't cheap. It cost the dear Son of God His very life.

Only cheap, tawdry things have a price tag on them. The best things in life are free—the air we breathe, the stars at night, the wonder of human love. But the greatest gift of all is our salvation, purchased for us by Jesus Christ. "Thanks be to God for His indescribable gift!" (2 Corinthians 9:15).

GRACE
FOR THE MOMENT

*Inspirational
Thoughts for Each Day
of the Year*

Max Lucado

At Home with God

If people love me, they will obey my teaching.
My Father will love them, and we will come
to them and make our home with them.

JOHN 14:23 NCV

God wants to be your dwelling place. He has no interest in being a weekend getaway or a Sunday bungalow or a summer cottage. Don't consider using God as a vacation cabin or an eventual retirement home. He wants you under his roof now and always. He wants to be your mailing address, your point of reference; he wants to be your home. . . .

For many this is a new thought. We think of God as a deity to discuss, not a place to dwell. We think of God as a mysterious miracle worker, not a house to live in. We think of God as a creator to call on, not a home to reside in. But our Father wants to be much more. He wants to be the one in whom "we live and move and have our being" (Acts 17:28 NIV).

The Great House of God

The Only Path

I am the way, and the truth, and the life.
The only way to the Father is through me.

JOHN 14:6 NCV

Tolerance. A prized virtue today. The ability to be understanding of those with whom you differ is a sign of sophistication. Jesus, too, was a champion of tolerance:

- Tolerant of the disciples when they doubted.
- Tolerant of the crowds when they misunderstood.
- Tolerant of us when we fall.

But there is one area where Jesus was intolerant. There was one area where he was unindulgent and dogmatic. . . .

As far as he was concerned, when it comes to salvation, there aren't several roads . . . there is only one road. . . . There aren't several paths . . . there is only one path. And that path is Jesus himself.

That is why it is so hard for people to believe in Jesus. It's much easier to consider him one of several options rather than the option. But such a philosophy is no option.

A Gentle Thunder

God's Passion and Plan

Your word is like a lamp
for my feet and a light for my path.
PSALM 119:105 NCV

The purpose of the Bible is simply to proclaim God's plan to save His children. It asserts that man is lost and needs to be saved. And it communicates the message that Jesus is the God in the flesh sent to save his children.

Though the Bible was written over sixteen centuries by at least forty authors, it has one central theme—salvation through faith in Christ. Begun by Moses in the lonely desert of Arabia and finished by John on the lonely Isle of Patmos, it is held together by a strong thread: God's passion and God's plan to save His children.

What a vital truth! Understanding the purpose of the Bible is like setting the compass in the right direction. Calibrate it correctly and you'll journey safely. But fail to set it, and who knows where you'll end up.

"How to Study the Bible"

Found, Called, and Adopted

It is not the healthy people
who need a doctor, but the sick. . . .
I did not come to invite good people
but to invite sinners.

MATTHEW 9:12–13 NCV

God didn't look at our frazzled lives and say, "I'll die for you when you deserve it."

No, despite our sin, in the face of our rebellion, he chose to adopt us. And for God, there's no going back. His grace is a come-as-you-are promise from a one-of-a-kind King. You've been found, called, and adopted; so trust your Father and claim this verse as your own: "God showed his love for us in this way: Christ died for us while we were still sinners" (Romans 5:8). And you never again have to wonder who your father is—you've been adopted by God and are therefore an "heir of God through Christ" (Galatians 4:7).

In the Grip of Grace

ANNE GRAHAM LOTZ

MEDITATING DAILY ON GOD'S WORD

GOD LOVES EVERYONE

Whoever confesses that Jesus is the Son of God,
God abides in him, and he in God.

1 JOHN 4:15 NKJV

God loves each and every person who has ever been born into the human race! God loves:

the Eskimo living in an ice hut,
the Chinese living in a bamboo lodge,
the African living in a mud hut,
the homeless living in a cardboard box,
the Bedouin living in a tent,
the Indian living in a teepee,
the royals living in a palace,
the slum dweller living in a housing project,

God loves the whole world! God loves you! And God loves even me!

Nowhere in the Bible does it say that everyone on Planet Earth is a child of God. But the Bible does say God loves everyone on Planet Earth, and we can call God our Father when we come to Him in a personal relationship through faith in His Son.

God's Story

THE FOUNDATION FOR FAITH

"Everyone who hears these words of mine
and puts them into practice is like
a wise man who built his house on the rock."

MATTHEW 7:24 NIV

On what foundation are you building your life? What feels right? What works? What everyone else is doing?

How stable is your foundation? When an unexpected crisis comes, will your life remain firm and steadfast, or will it all collapse?

The foundation of faith in Jesus Christ is one on which you and I can build our lives with confidence, knowing it will last, not only for our lifetimes but for all eternity as well.

Jesus said, "Everyone who hears these words of mine and puts them into practice is like a wise man who built his house on the rock. The rain came down, the streams rose, and the winds blew and beat against the house; yet it did not fall, because it had its foundation on the rock" (Matthew 7:24–25 NIV). So . . . check your foundation!

God's Story

CREATED TO KNOW GOD

*"Now this is eternal life: that they may know you, the only
true God, and Jesus Christ, whom you have sent."*

JOHN 17:3 NIV

Man was created
to walk and talk with God,
to love and obey God,
to listen to and learn from God,
to glorify and enjoy God forever!
Jesus defined our meaning for existence when He
prayed, "Now this is eternal life: that they may know you,
the only true God, and Jesus Christ, whom you have
sent." Knowing God in a personal and permanent
relationship is the ultimate human experience. Knowing
God is the meaning of human life. It is the reason for our
existence. It was the completion of all the changes God
made in the environment in the beginning. And it is the
completion of all the changes God is making in your life
at the present.

Get to know Him and discover the real meaning of
life.

God's Story

COME TO HIM

There is no one righteous, not even one.
ROMANS 3:10 NIV

In their pride, the builders of Babel (Genesis 11:4) assumed they could work their way into God's Presence and He would accept them on the basis of what they had done. They were wrong then, and they are still wrong today.

God has said that "All our righteous acts are like filthy rags," (Isaiah 64:6 NIV) and "There is no one righteous, not even one," (Romans 3:10 NIV) and "Without holiness no one will see the Lord" (Hebrews 12:14 NIV). So how does one get into heaven? Jesus gave clear instructions, "Not everyone . . . will enter the kingdom of heaven, but only he who does the will of my Father who is in heaven," (Matthew 7:21 NIV) and "I am the way and the truth and the life. No one comes to the Father except through me" (John 14:6 NIV). All religions are man's rebellious, prideful attempt to get around God's stated will and Word. Instead of arguing with Him, just come to Him through Jesus!

God's Story

Truth

FOR TODAY

A Daily Touch of God's Grace

John
MacArthur

THE POWER OF THE GOSPEL

For I am not ashamed of the gospel of Christ,
for it is the power of God to salvation.

ROMANS 1:16 NKJV

People want to change. All advertising is based on the presupposition that people want things different from the way they are. They want to look better, feel better, think better, and live better. They want to change their lives but, except from an external standpoint, they are unable to do so.

Only the gospel of Jesus Christ has the power to change people and deliver them from sin, from Satan, from judgment, from death, and from hell. Acts 4:12 says, "Nor is there salvation in any other, for there is no other name under heaven given among men by which we must be saved." And that name is Jesus Christ.

So God's Word, which is all about Jesus Christ, can do for us what we cannot do for ourselves. We are sinful and unable to remedy our condition, but from God comes the incredible, limitless power that can transform our lives.

No More Bad News

Separated to the gospel of God.

ROMANS 1:1 NKJV

 Thousands of babies are born every day into a world filled with bad news. The term bad news has become a colloquialism to describe our era.

Why is there so much bad news? It's simple. The bad news that occurs on a larger scale is only the multiplication of what is occurring on an individual level. The power that makes for bad news is sin.

With so much bad news, can there really be any good news? Yes! The good news is that sin can be dealt with. You don't have to be selfish. Guilt and anxiety can be alleviated. There is meaning to life and hope of life after death. The apostle Paul says in Romans 1:1 that the good news is the gospel. It is the good news that man's sin can be forgiven, guilt can be removed, life can have meaning, and a hopeful future can be a reality.

Fulfilling the Law

Therefore you shall be perfect,
just as your Father in heaven is perfect.

MATTHEW 5:48 NKJV

Jesus faced much opposition during His ministry when He didn't agree with contemporary Jewish theology (Matthew 15:1–3). Because it was hypocritical, He denied the Pharisees' so-called devotion.

Many in His day were saying, "Is Jesus saying new truth? Is He really speaking for God? He doesn't say what the Pharisees say. He, in fact, says the opposite of what we're taught."

Jesus said, "Do not think that I came to destroy the Law or the Prophets. I did not come to destroy but to fulfill" (Matthew 5:17). Jesus did not condemn Old Testament law, but He did condemn the tradition that had been built up around it. The religious leaders had so perverted God's law that Jesus declared, "I say to you, that unless your righteousness exceeds the righteousness of the scribes and Pharisees, you will by no means enter the kingdom of heaven" (v. 20).

Whose righteousness are you depending on? Your own or Christ's?

Undeserved Favor

Where sin abounded, grace abounded much more.

ROMANS 5:20 NKJV

 Salvation does not come by confirmation, communion, baptism, church membership, church attendance, trying to keep the Ten Commandments, or living out the Sermon on the Mount. It does not come by giving to charity or even by believing that there is a God. It does not come by simply being moral and respectable. Salvation does not even come by claiming to be a Christian. Salvation comes only when we receive by faith the gift of God's grace. Hell will be full of people who tried to reach heaven some other way.

The apostle Paul said, "The law entered that the offense might abound. But where sin abounded, grace abounded much more, so that as sin reigned in death, even so grace might reign through righteousness to eternal life through Jesus Christ our Lord" (Romans 5:20–21). The first provision of the gospel is grace, which is neither earned nor deserved.

Dr. Donald Grey Barnhouse said, "Love that gives upward is worship; love that goes outward is affection; love that stoops is grace." God has stooped to give us grace. Will you receive it?

WISDOM
for the way

WISE WORDS FOR BUSY PEOPLE

CHARLES R.
SWINDOLL

Magnificent Relief

I acknowledged my sin to You . . .
and You forgave the guilt of my sin.

PSALM 32:5 NASB

Like a cool, cleansing shower on a hot, sweaty day, God's forgiveness washes away not only sins but their tormenting guilt. God goes into the depths of our inner being and provides that magnificent relief that only He can bring: PEACE. . . .

If you are harboring some sin—if you are keeping hidden a few secret regions of wrong—don't expect to enjoy freedom from guilt, child of God. There is an unspoken axiom threaded through Scripture: secret sin cannot coexist with inner peace. Peace returns only when our sins are fully confessed and forsaken. Few grinds are more galling than the grind of an unforgiven conscience. It's awful! And few joys are more relieving than having our sins forgiven. It's wonderful!

Living Beyond the Daily Grind

Confident Contentment

Teach me to do Your will,
for You are my God;
let Your good Spirit lead
me on level ground.
PSALM 143:10 NASB

When Christ becomes our central focus—our reason for existence—contentment replaces our anxiety as well as our fears and insecurities. This cannot help but impact three of the most prevalent joy stealers in all of life.

1. *He broadens the dimensions of our circumstances.* This gives us new confidence. . . .

2. *He delivers us from preoccupation with others.* This causes our contentment level to rise. . . .

3. *He calms our fears regarding ourselves and our future.* This provides a burst of fresh hope on a daily basis.

Laugh Again

God Loves Us Still

I have loved you with an everlasting love;
therefore I have drawn you with lovingkindness.
JEREMIAH 31:3 NASB

From a distance, we dazzle; up close, we're tarnished. Put enough of us together and we may resemble an impressive mountain range. But when you get down into the shadowy crevices . . . the Alps we ain't.

That's why our Lord means so much to us. He is intimately acquainted with all our ways. Darkness and light are alike to Him. No one of us is hidden from His sight. All things are open and laid bare before Him: our darkest secret, our deepest shame, our stormy past, our worst thought, our hidden motive, our vilest imagination . . . even our vain attempts to cover the ugly with snow-white beauty.

He sees it all. He knows our frame. He remembers we are dust.

Best of all, He loves us still.

The Finishing Touch

The Urgency of the Hour

I am coming quickly;
hold fast what you have, so that
no one will take your crown.

REVELATION 3:11 NASB

If you live in the light of Christ's return each day of your life, it does wonders for your perspective. If you realize that you must give account for every idle word and action when you stand before the Lord Jesus, it does amazing things to your conduct. It also makes you recognize how many needless activities we get involved in on this earth. Sort of like rearranging the deck chairs on the *Titanic*. Don't bother! Don't get lost in insignificant details! He's coming soon! Recognize the urgency and the simplicity of the hour!

Hope Again

CRISIS SCRIPTURE GUIDE
(NKJV Translation)

ADDICTION. . . .

> Do not be entangled again with a yoke of bondage.
>
> *Galatians 5:1*

ANGER . . .

> Do not let the sun go down on your wrath.
>
> *Ephesians 4:26*

CHILDREN . . .

> Train up a child in the way he should go.
>
> *Proverbs 22:6*

CONFUSION. . .

> For God is not the author of confusion but of peace.
>
> *1 Corinthians 14:33*

DANGER . . .

> God is our refuge and strength, a very present help in trouble.
>
> *Psalm 46:1*

DEATH. . .

> God will wipe away every tear from their eyes; there shall be no more death, nor sorrow, nor crying.
>
> *Revelation 21:4*

DECISION-MAKING . . .

> Trust in the LORD with all your heart, and lean not on your own understanding.
>
> *Proverbs 3:5*

DEPRESSION. . .

> In everything give thanks, for this is the will of God.
>
> *1 Thessalonians 5:18*

DESPAIR. . .

> Wait on the LORD; be of good courage, and He shall strengthen your heart.
>
> *Psalm 27:14*

DISCOURAGEMENT. . .

> Be of good courage, and He shall strengthen your heart. *Psalm 31:24*

DIVORCE . . .

> Therefore what God has joined together, let not man separate. *Mark 10:9*

EXHAUSTION . . .

> Cast your burden on the LORD, and He shall sustain you. *Psalm 55:22*

FAILURE . . .

> We know that all things work together for good to those who love God. *Romans 8:28*

FEAR . . .

> Fear not, for I am with you; be not dismayed, for I am your God. *Isaiah 41:10*

FINANCIAL TROUBLE. . .

> My God shall supply all your need according to His riches in glory. *Philippians 4:19*

GRIEF. . .

>Yes, though I walk through the valley of the shadow of death, I will fear no evil; For You are with me.
>
>*Psalm 23:4*

ILLNESS. . .

>The prayer of faith will save the sick, and the Lord will raise him up.
>
>*James 5:15*

ISOLATION. . .

>For I am persuaded that neither death nor life, not angels nor principalities nor powers, nor things present nor things to come, nor height nor depth, nor any other created thing, shall be able to separate us from the love of God.
>
>*Romans 8:38–39*

LONELINESS. . .

>For the LORD will not forsake His people.
>
>*1 Samuel 12:22*

LUST. . .

>Walk in the Spirit, and you shall not fulfill the lust of the flesh.
>
>*Galatians 5:16*

MARRIAGE. . .

>Therefore a man shall leave his father and mother and be joined to his wife, and they shall become one flesh.
>
>*Genesis 2:24*

OLD AGE. . .

> My flesh and my heart fail; But God is the strength of
> my heart and my portion forever.
>
> *Psalm 73:26*

REBELLION. . .

> Do not present your members as instruments of
> unrighteousness to sin, but present yourselves to God.
>
> *Romans 6:13*

REJECTION. . .

> He heals the brokenhearted and binds up their
> wounds.
>
> *Psalm 147:3*

SALVATION . . .

> For God so loved the world that He gave His only
> begotten Son, that whoever believes in Him should
> not perish but have everlasting life.
>
> *John 3:16*

STRESS. . .

> They cried out to the LORD in their trouble, And He
> delivered them out of their distresses.
>
> *Psalm 107:6*

SUFFERING. . .

> Christ also suffered for us, leaving us an example, that
> you should follow His steps.
>
> *1 Peter 2:21*

TEMPTATION. . .

Blessed is the man who endures temptation; for when he has been approved, he will receive the crown of life which the Lord has promised to those who love Him.

James 1:12

TRIALS. . .

The righteous cry out, and the LORD hears, and delivers them out of all their troubles.

Psalm 34:17

UNCERTAINTY. . .

He who has begun a good work in you will complete it until the day of Jesus Christ.

Philippians 1:6

WEAKNESS. . .

I can do all things through Christ who strengthens me.

Philippians 4:13

WORRY. . .

Be anxious for nothing, but in everything by prayer and supplication, with thanksgiving, let your requests be made known to God.

Philippians 4:6

VISIT YOUR LOCAL CHRISTIAN BOOKSTORE TO PURCHASE ONE OF THE FOLLOWING **DEVOTIONALS**

HOPE FOR EACH DAY
by Billy Graham
ISBN: 978-0-8499-9620-7

THE JOY OF MY HEART
by Anne Graham Lotz
ISBN: 978-1-4041-0116-6